IN THE ZONE

HOCKEY

ROBB JOHNSTONE

Published by Weigl Publishers Inc.
350 5th Avenue, Suite 3304, PMB 6G
New York, NY 10118-0069

Website: www.weigl.com

Library of Congress Cataloging-in-Publication Data

Johnstone, Robb.
 Hockey / Robb Johnstone.
    p. cm. -- (In the Zone)
 Includes index.
 ISBN 978-1-60596-130-9 (hard cover : alk. paper) -- ISBN 978-1-60596-131-6 (soft cover : alk. paper)
 1. Hockey--Juvenile literature. I. Title.
 GV847.25.J64 2010
 796.962--dc22

                              2009005607

Printed in China
1 2 3 4 5 6 7 8 9 13 12 11 10 09

Weigl acknowledges Getty Images as its primary image supplier for this title.

Illustrations
Kenzie Browne: pages 9, 10 Left.

Heather C. Hudak Project Coordinator
Terry Paulhus Design
Kenzie Browne Layout

CONTENTS

Hockey is a game of speed, skill, and physical strength.

P eople disagree on who invented hockey and where it started. Some argue that Aboriginal Peoples first played a similar game in Canada. However, the person most often credited with inventing hockey is James Creighton. He took part in the first organized hockey game in 1875. A Canadian university student, W.F. Robertson, established the first set of rules.

In the early 1900s, hockey players wore very little padding and protective gear.

At first, people played hockey on frozen lakes and rivers. It was only played in countries that have a cold climate, such as Canada. Today, people can play hockey anywhere because of indoor ice rinks.

There are two teams in a hockey game. Each team tries to put a hard rubber puck into the other team's net. This is called scoring a **goal**. When time runs out, the game is over. The team that scores the most goals wins.

Sports Facts

To brush up on your hockey knowledge, surf to www.exploratorium.edu/hockey.

A long time ago, a hockey player only needed a sheet of ice, a pair of skates, a stick, and a puck. Some people still play hockey this way. It is called "shinny." This is a good name because you can get many bruises on your shins if you do not wear equipment.

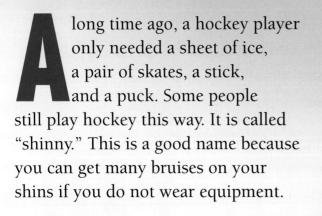

A hockey jersey is often large. It has to fit elbow and shoulder pads underneath it.

Players wear thick gloves. They protect the player's hands and keep them warm. Goalies use gloves to help them block shots.

Players glide on the ice on skates. Skates have sharp blades on the bottoms. The boots are made of leather or light plastic.

Hockey pants are like long shorts. Players wear long wool socks or long underwear under the pants. Shin pads are worn under their socks.

Players use sticks to control the puck. Many people wrap tape around the **blade** of the stick. This helps them handle the puck better. Goalies use different sticks than other players. Their sticks are wider at the bottom to help them block shots better.

Pucks are small disks made of rubber. Players pass the puck to each other and try to put it in the other team's net. In professional hockey, pucks are frozen before being used. This stops them from bouncing too much on the ice.

Most pucks are made of hard, black rubber.

Players wear helmets, and often face guards, all the time. This helps protect them from injuries. Goaltenders, or goalies, wear special helmets that provide extra protection.

Goaltenders use blockers to stop shots. Blockers are pads worn on the goalie's stick hand. They use them to knock the puck away from the net.

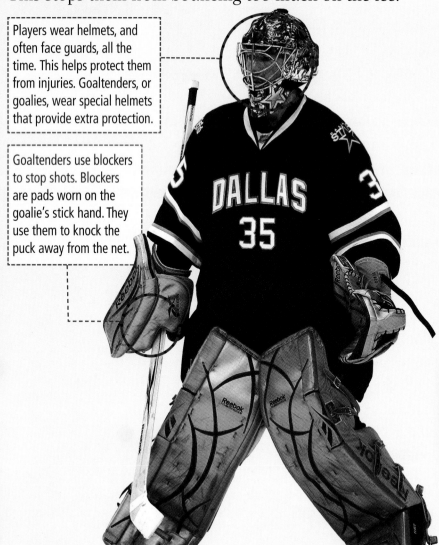

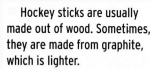

Hockey sticks are usually made out of wood. Sometimes, they are made from graphite, which is lighter.

A goalpost is located at each end of the ice.

7

A hockey rink is a big sheet of ice with a net at each end. High boards surround the ice. There are lines and circles on the ice that are important to the rules of the game.

A thick red line is found in the middle of the ice, and there are two thin red lines near the ends. Two blue lines are painted between the red lines.

The circles on the ice show where the officials drop the puck to start play. When the official drops the puck, it is called a **face-off** because a player from one team faces a player from the other team. They both try to knock the puck to their teammates. As a result, the circles are called face-off circles.

Winning the face-off takes skill and speed. A player has to touch the puck before the other team.

The **boards** around the rink are designed to keep the puck and players inside. There is usually glass or wire **mesh** that sits on top of the boards. This keeps the puck from flying out and hitting people in the stands.

There are two places, called benches, for players on each team to sit. Special gates at the benches allow players to go onto the ice. As well, there are two **penalty** boxes where players go when they break the rules.

Sports Venues

To learn more about a hockey rink, check out www.howstuffworks.com/ice-rink.htm.

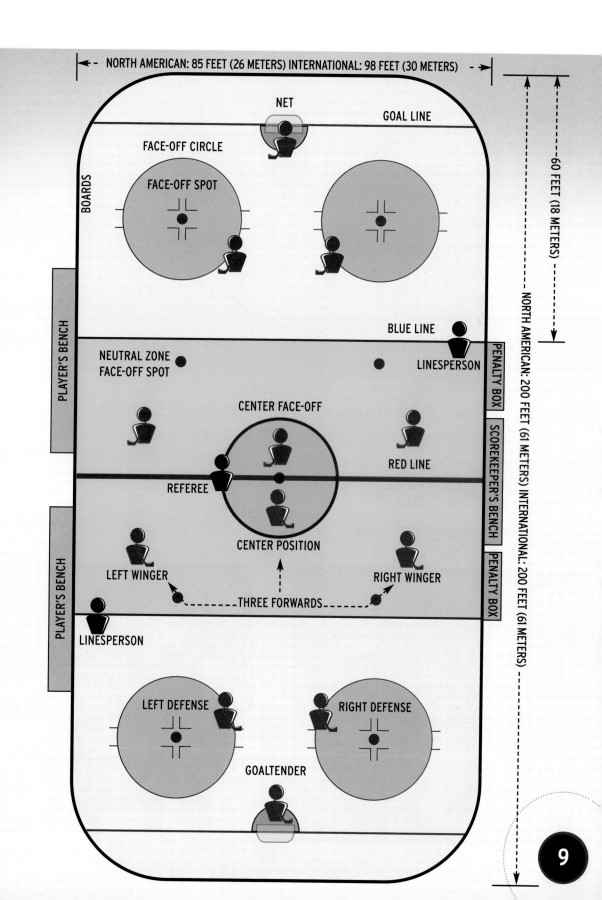

NORTH AMERICAN: 85 FEET (26 METERS) INTERNATIONAL: 98 FEET (30 METERS)

NET

GOAL LINE

FACE-OFF CIRCLE

FACE-OFF SPOT

BOARDS

60 FEET (18 METERS)

BLUE LINE

LINESPERSON

NEUTRAL ZONE
FACE-OFF SPOT

PENALTY BOX

CENTER FACE-OFF

PLAYER'S BENCH

SCOREKEEPER'S BENCH

RED LINE

NORTH AMERICAN: 200 FEET (61 METERS) INTERNATIONAL: 200 FEET (61 METERS)

REFEREE

PENALTY BOX

CENTER POSITION

LEFT WINGER

RIGHT WINGER

PLAYER'S BENCH

THREE FORWARDS

LINESPERSON

LEFT DEFENSE

RIGHT DEFENSE

GOALTENDER

9

Players have to follow the rules. They cannot use their sticks to trip or hit other players. They also cannot hold another player back using their hands or sticks. To make sure everyone will be safe, players must keep their sticks below the shoulders. If they do not, they can be called for **high-sticking**.

Players cannot stand by their opponent's net and wait for the puck. If they do, they will be called **offside**. Offside is when a player moves across the other team's blue line before the puck does. Players cannot pass the puck across the blue and center lines. This is an offside pass.

Icing is when a player shoots the puck from his or her end of the rink. It crosses the goal line on the other end without anyone touching it. The puck is then brought back to where it was shot originally.

Referee Signals

Referees use hand signals to show calls. These are a few examples.

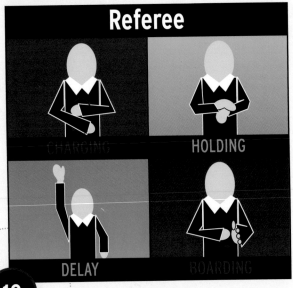

The referee uses his or her hands to signal a penalty and to direct the hockey game.

These rules are designed to make sure the game is played fairly and to keep players from being hurt. During the game, a referee watches out for players who break the rules.

If a player breaks a rule, the referee blows a whistle and stops the game. Sometimes, a player is sent to the penalty box for breaking a rule. That player's team must play with one fewer player. This gives the other team an advantage, so players are encouraged to always follow the rules. In professional hockey, the referee is joined by two linespeople, who help **enforce** the rules.

Players must wait until their time in the penalty box is finished before re-joining the game.

Hockey can be a very rough game. This is why players wear protective padding and a helmet.

There are three positions in hockey. These are goaltender, defender, and forward. Each team puts one goalie, two defenders, and three forwards on the ice at one time.

Goalies stay in front of the net and keep their opponents from scoring. They wear special equipment to protect them from shots. It takes a great deal of bravery to be a goaltender. A puck shot from a stick can travel at more than 100 miles (161 kilometers) per hour. Goalies usually stay on the ice for the entire game. Other players play in **shifts**.

Players have to use their muscles to keep control of the puck.

The goalie is the last line of defense when a player from the opposing team is trying to score a goal.

The defender's job is similar to the goalie's. Both try to keep other players from scoring. For this reason, defenders usually stay close to their net. Defenders can go anywhere on the ice, so they can also score goals.

A forward's job is to score goals. There is a center forward, a right wing, and a left wing. They all try to break through the other team's defense and take shots on the net.

Forwards use their skating speed to move the puck toward the net.

When the puck is close to the net, players rush to help their goalie.

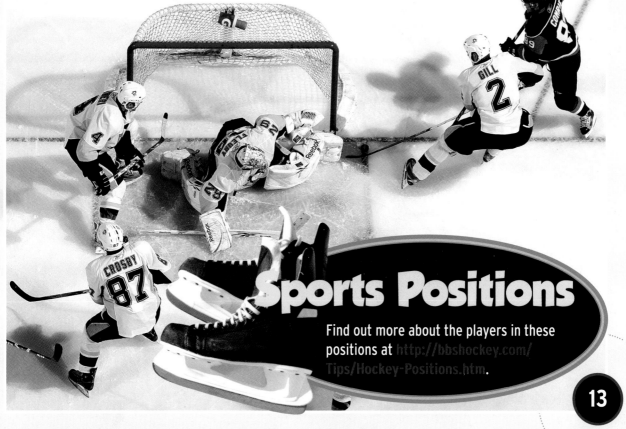

Sports Positions

Find out more about the players in these positions at http://bbshockey.com/Tips/Hockey-Positions.htm.

When they first start playing hockey, players practice skating and decide which position they want to play. As they get older, they get better at hockey and move up from one level to the next—from Mite to Squirt to PeeWee to Bantam.

Players who continue to play into their teens may play on Junior teams. They may also choose to play on college or university teams. These leagues attract attention from professional teams. Other leagues, including the American Hockey League (AHL) and the International Hockey League (IHL), act as farm teams for the National Hockey League (NHL).

Practice is important at any age.

NHL teams work hard all season to try to reach the playoffs.

Every year, the professional teams get together to choose the young players they want. This is called a **draft**. Each team takes turns picking players until all available players have been chosen. It is a big thrill for players who are chosen first overall. That usually means they are headed for success in the NHL.

Every player in the NHL wants to win the Stanley Cup. The Stanley Cup is the oldest award for professional athletes in North America. It was first given out in 1894. This award is given to the top team at the end of the championship playoffs.

Winning the Stanley Cup is one of the greatest achievements in a player's career.

National teams represent their home countries in international competition.

Hockey has many past heroes. Many of these heroes inspired today's professionals to play the game.

Maurice (Rocket) Richard

POSITION: Right Wing
TEAM: Montreal Canadiens
SIGNED TO THE NHL: 1942

CAREER FACTS:
- Maurice was known as "The Rocket."
- During his career, Maurice won the Stanley Cup with the Canadiens eight times.
- Maurice was one of the game's greatest goal scorers. At the end of his career, he had scored 544 goals. This was a record at the time.
- Maurice was the first player to score 50 goals in one season. At this time, teams only played 50 games in each season.

Gordie Howe

POSITION: Right Wing
TEAM: Detroit Red Wings
SIGNED TO THE NHL: 1946

CAREER FACTS:
- Gordie's career lasted from when he was a teenager until he was in his fifties.
- Gordie was known as "Mr. Hockey."
- Gordie's points record of 1,850 lasted until 1989. It was broken by Wayne Gretzky, who was Gordie's biggest fan.
- Gordie stayed in hockey for so long that he played on the same team as his two sons.
- In his career, Gordie played 2,421 games–scoring 1,071 goals, with 1,518 assists. This gave him a professional total of 2,589 points.

Bobby Orr

POSITION: Defender
TEAM: Boston Bruins, Chicago Blackhawks
SIGNED TO THE NHL: 1966

CAREER FACTS:

- Bobby changed how people thought of defense players. He was a powerful defender, but he could score goals, too.
- Bobby was the first defender to score more than 40 goals in a season.
- Bobby was the first defender to score 100 points and to win the overall scoring title.
- Bobby was the first hockey player in the world to earn $1 million.

Wayne Gretzky

POSITION: Center
TEAM: Edmonton Oilers, L.A. Kings, St. Louis Blues, New York Rangers
SIGNED TO THE NHL: 1979

CAREER FACTS:

- In 1989, Wayne broke Gordie Howe's points record. Wayne ended his career with 2,856 points.
- Wayne was a member of the Edmonton Oilers in the 1980s, when the team dominated the game.
- Wayne holds 61 NHL records.
- In the 1982-1983 **season**, Wayne scored an incredible 92 goals.
- Wayne made Los Angeles hockey fans excited about hockey when he was traded to the L.A. Kings in 1988.

The hockey stars of today have fans cheering in the stands.

Sidney Crosby

POSITION: Center
TEAM: Pittsburg Penguins
SIGNED TO THE NHL: 2005

CAREER FACTS:

- At the age of 20, Sidney became the youngest team captain in NHL history.
- He became the youngest player in NHL history to have two 100-point seasons.
- Sidney has been nicknamed "The Next One," referring to the fact that he was the most highly regarded draft pick in hockey history. Many people thought he would be the next Wayne Gretzky, or The Great One.
- When Wayne Gretzky was asked if a player might one day break some of his NHL scoring records, Gretzky said that Sidney Crosby had the skill.

Alexander Ovechkin

POSITION: Left Wing
TEAM: Washington Capitals
SIGNED TO THE NHL: 2004

CAREER FACTS:

- In 2008, Alexander won the Lester B. Pearson Award, Hart memorial trophy, Rocket Richard Trophy, and Art Ross Trophy. He was the first player in NHL history to win all four awards.
- The Florida Panthers wanted to draft him in the 2003 NHL Entry Draft, but his birthday was two days after the cut-off, making him two days too young to play in the NHL.
- Alexander finished the 2007-2008 season as the leader in points, with 112 points and 65 goals.
- He holds the NHL record for the fastest overtime goal-six seconds.

Joe Thornton

POSITION: Right Wing
TEAM: San Jose Sharks
SIGNED TO THE NHL: 1997

CAREER FACTS:

- Joe was the first overall draft in the first round of the 1997 NHL draft.
- He is only the third player in NHL history to have consecutive 90-assist seasons.
- Joe was the first Sharks player to win the Hart Memorial Trophy and the Art Ross Trophy.
- He holds the NHL record for points in a season by a player that was on two different teams in one season.

Paul Kariya

POSITION: Left Wing
TEAM: St. Louis Blues
SIGNED TO THE NHL: 1994

CAREER FACTS:

- Paul has won the NHL All-Star Roster five times.
- Paul has scored more than 100 points in a season twice in his career.
- Paul was a runner-up for the Calder Trophy, which is given to the league's best rookie.

Sports Heroes

Keep track of your favorite hockey heroes at www.nhl.com.

Hockey players need to eat right so they can play hard. That starts with daily servings from all the food groups, including breads and cereals, fruits and vegetables, meats and proteins, and milk and milk products.

It is important for athletes to take in enough **calories**. Athletes, including hockey players, use up more energy than people who do not exercise as much. Athletes need to choose the foods they eat wisely. Food can affect the way athletes perform.

Water is also very important. The body should always be properly **hydrated**. Sports drinks help to get liquids into the body quickly during practices and games. Players should also drink plenty of water every day, both while exercising and while resting.

Pasta is an excellent source of carbohydrates.

Fruit also provides nutrients the body needs to keep healthy and active.

Sports Health

Learn more about eating healthy by visiting http://mypyramid.gov.

Most hockey players are extremely good athletes. Their muscles are strong, and they can exercise hard for long periods of time. To avoid injuries, they stretch their muscles well before and after a game or practice.

Players must be able to skate at full speed for quick bursts, and they must be able to play an entire game. That means hockey players need two different types of training. They need one to make them fast and another to build their **endurance**.

Hockey players often train with inline skates, or rollerblades. This makes them stronger skaters.

Bicycling and long-distance running are two activities athletes can perform to build up their endurance. Sprinting is a good way to build up speed. This keeps them in shape over the summer.

It is important to stretch as part of warming up to play a sport.

Test your knowledge of this exciting sport by trying to answer these hockey brain teasers!

Q Who made the first set of rules for hockey?

A W.F. Robertson established the first set of rules.

Q Who is the youngest team captain in NHL history?

A Sidney Crosby is the youngest team captain in NHL history.

Q What is the Stanley Cup?

A The Stanley Cup is the oldest award for professional athletes in North America. This award is given to the top team at the end of the championship playoffs.

Q What is a forward's job?

A A forward's job is to score goals.

Q What do goalie sticks look like?

A Goalie sticks are wider at the bottom to help them block shots better.

Q Who was the first defender to score more than 40 goals in a season?

A Bobby Orr was the first defender to score more than 40 goals in a season.

Glossary

blade: the thin, flat part of a stick

boards: the barrier around a rink that keeps the puck and players inside

calories: energy values of food

draft: process used to select players for sports teams; the team that finishes in last place chooses first in the draft

endurance: the ability to continue an activity for a long time

enforce: to make sure rules are followed

face-off: when the referee drops the puck between two players

goal: when the whole puck crosses the red goal line and goes in the net

high-sticking: holding the blade of the hockey stick above shoulder level

hydrated: combined with water

mesh: an arrangement of interlocking links that form a net

offside: being beyond an allowed area or line before the puck

penalty: when a player breaks a rule, that player is sent to the penalty box, and the team plays with fewer players

season: the length of time between opening day and the last playoff game. The professional hockey season begins in October and ends in June.

shifts: groups of players who play together for a set period of time and then come off the ice; another shift of players takes their place

Index